These Forty Days
Understanding the Symbols and Practices of Lent

Timothy McCanna

One Liguori Drive
Liguori MO 63057-9999
314.464.2500

Imprimi Potest:
James Shea, C.SS.R.
Provincial, St. Louis Province
The Redemptorists

Imprimatur:
Monsignor Maurice F. Byrne
Vice Chancellor, Archdiocese of St. Louis

Copyright © 1992, Liguori Publications
Printed in the United States of America
98 99 00   8 7 6 5

All rights reserved. No part of this pamphlet may be reproduced, stored in a retrieval system, or transmitted without the written permission of Liguori Publications.

Scripture selections are take from THE NEW AMERICAN BIBLE WITH REVISED NEW TESTAMENT, copyright © 1986, by the Confraternity of Christian Doctrine, Washington, D.C., and are used with permission. All rights reserved.

Excerpts from VATICAN II: THE CONCILIAR AND POST CONCILIAR DOCUMENTS, edited by Austin Flannery, O.P., copyright © 1988, Costello Publishing company, Northport, NY, are used by permission of the publisher. All rights reserved.

Excerpts from the English translation of *The Roman Missal*, copyright © 1973, International Committee on English in the Liturgy (ICEL), are used with permission. All rights reserved.

Cover design by Pam Hummelsheim

These Forty Days
Understanding the Symbols and Practices of Lent

Timothy McCanna

Introduction

As a child, did you ever walk into an empty old Gothic church? Do you recall the mysterious feeling it evoked? In the middle of the week, even on a sunny day, it was cool inside, and the aroma of incense and old wood and wax pervaded the atmosphere. The sun shining through the stained-glass windows captured floating dust motes in red and blue beams of light. The vaulted ceiling seemed so high. Every statue and picture seemed to have a story to tell, if only you could find someone to explain it.

Just as the sights, sounds, tastes, and smells of our childhood can bring back all sorts of memories, the Church uses all the senses to teach and celebrate God's message of love to us. Saint Thomas Aquinas reminded us that the fingerprints of God are found all over creation and that by understanding creation we come to a better knowledge of the Creator. Catholicism has used art, sacramentals, music, vestments, flowers, incense, and images as ways of speaking to the whole person.

Each of the liturgical seasons has its own set of symbols to help us celebrate the religious meaning of that season. What do you think of when you hear the word *Lent* — "giving up" candy, desserts, snacks, or alcohol; attending daily Mass; making the Stations of the Cross; praying the rosary; meditating on Jesus' passion and death; seeing statues in church covered with purple cloths; ashes and palms?

In this pamphlet we will take a look at some of the symbols and practices associated with Lent. Some of them may have been a part of your Lenten observance since childhood; others may be new and unfamiliar to you. A deeper understanding of these special images and practices can help make the celebration of Lent a better preparation for Easter.

Lent…Why Forty Days?

The organ had just intoned the seasonal hymn "These Forty Days of Lent." Only a few bars into the familiar melody, the youngster in the front pew asked, "Why is it forty days?"

Good question.

The word *lent* comes from an early English word that refers to the lengthening of daylight hours during spring. The season of Lent has long been the Church's preparation for Easter. It developed long before the separation of the Eastern Catholic Churches from the Roman Catholic Church and was simply called "the forty days" in the Greek and Latin languages.

The number forty has a symbolic meaning in Scripture and occurs in several passages in both the Old and New Testaments. During the great Flood in Noah's time, it rained for forty days and forty nights. After departing from Egypt, the Israelites wandered in the desert for forty years. Elijah walked forty days to the mountain of God, Horeb.

The gospels of Matthew, Mark, and Luke all tell us that Jesus spent forty days in the desert after his baptism in the Jordan River. "Jesus…was led by the Spirit into the desert for forty days, to be tempted by the devil" (Luke 4:1-2). These gospel passages are used in the Liturgy of the Word on the first Sunday of Lent.

Jesus' desert experience reminded the gospel communities of the Israelites who were freed from Egyptian slavery only to wander in the desert for forty years on their way to the Promised Land. During that time, they were tempted and they sinned. Jesus reversed that failure. The gospels of Matthew and Luke list three temptations, in slightly different variations. Jesus is tempted to turn stones into bread, to jump from the roof of the Temple to show that his Father will protect him, and to worship Satan in return for political power to accomplish his mission. By his faithfulness to his Father, Jesus encountered, but overcame, the same temptations presented to the Israelites in the desert.

The practice of preparing for Easter with six weeks of prayer, fasting, almsgiving, and penance seems to have its origin in the late fourth century. Government persecution of Christians and official refusal to recognize the Church prior to that time may explain the lack of historical evidence for any earlier Lenten practices. Apparently, the preparation for Easter was limited to catechumens in the final stages of preparation for baptism at the Easter Vigil and to members of the faithful who joined them out of solidarity. Available records indicate a fast of one or two days before Easter or perhaps a forty-hour fast.

The connection of the Sunday liturgies of Lent to the preparation of adult catechumens for the sacrament of baptism has been re-established through the revival of the Rite of Christian Initiation of Adults. On several Sundays of Lent there are special prayers for those who will be baptized at the Easter Vigil.

When the practice of Lent finally emerged, it was not exactly in its present form in the Roman Catholic Church. Originally, there was a seven-week observance in the Eastern rite Church and a six-week observance in the Roman Catholic Church. Neither Church counted Sundays as part of Lent, and the Eastern Catholics didn't count Saturdays. Some time later, the Roman Church added Ash Wednesday and the rest of that week to make exactly forty days.

If we realize that the development of the Lenten season took place over several centuries, we can appreciate even more fully the religious practices of our heritage and those who contributed to it. Perhaps we will also be willing to accept a greater sense of responsibility to hand on that tradition to future generations.

Fasting With a Purpose

The Book of Jonah tells of a reluctant prophet who did not want to preach repentance to the people of Nineveh, whom he hated. He wanted them to be punished, so he tried to get out of God's command to preach to them. His tricks did not work, however. When Jonah preached repentance to the pagan Ninevites, their king responded by telling his people to fast, dress in sackcloth, and turn from their evil ways. Only in this way would the Lord have mercy on them.

Fasting, the practice of limiting the amount of food and drink that one consumes, is an ancient form of penance common to all the great religions. Fasting is not just a religious practice, however. It has been used as an expression of political protest and as an exercise for dieting and better health. Abstaining from various types of nourishment is said to purify one's system. Some of us don't mind the fact that fasting can help us take off a few pounds during Lent.

Fasting for religious purposes is a practice of self-discipline that has been employed over the centuries as an aid to concentration in prayer. However, like nearly any other kind of religious practice, fasting can be subject to abuses. It can be a sham — an external sign without inner conversion of heart. In Israel, where fasting was a prescribed practice, the prophet Isaiah (chapter 58) spoke of God's displeasure when the people fasted and still continued their sinful ways. God calls for a fast that will free the oppressed, feed and clothe the needy, and embrace the poor. Jesus also warned against fasting that is done only to impress others. (See Matthew 6:16.)

The discipline of fasting has always been a part of Church life, but the particulars have varied from century to century. Pope Paul VI revised the rules of fast and abstinence in 1966. The 1983 updated Code of Canon Law (#1251-1253) provides the regulations that we observe today.

Pope Paul VI emphasized self-denial for the sake of interior conversion. He noted that work, family relationships, ill health — the circumstances of daily living — are able to teach us patience and self-discipline. Prayer and works of charity must be combined with fast and abstinence for genuine Christian living.

Lenten regulations for fast and abstinence vary slightly in the United States and Canada, as canon law allows national conferences of bishops to determine area customs (#1253). The law of abstinence prohibits the eating of meat for all those fourteen years of age and over. The law of fast allows only one full meal a day, but does not prohibit taking some food in the morning and evening; in addition, eating between meals is prohibited. Fasting binds those from age eighteen up to midnight between their fifty-ninth birthday and the next day. In the United States, all Fridays of Lent are days of abstinence. In Canada, all Fridays throughout the year are days of abstinence, but special acts of charity or piety may be substituted. In both countries, Ash Wednesday and Good Friday are the required days of fasting and abstinence.

Making Sense of Lenten Symbols

The season of Lent, like all the liturgical seasons, appeals not only to the intellect but also to the senses. The Genesis account of creation portrays God creating light and darkness, water, vegetation, animals, and human beings. God sees all creation and declares that it is good. Our gifts of sight, taste, touch, smell, and hearing enable us to appreciate color, flavor, texture, odor, and sound. God's creation is filled with these qualities, and they speak to us of the goodness of creation.

In *The Constitution on the Sacred Liturgy,* the Second Vatican Council clearly stated the Church's belief in the value of the arts. "Of their nature the arts are directed toward expressing in some way the infinite beauty of God in works made by human hands" (#122). It calls the Church a patron of the fine arts.

In the sacraments and sacramentals of the Church, we use both words and elements. Water, oil, fire, salt, palms, colors, and ashes — all of these speak to the whole person.

Color: The colors of the vestments and the decorations in the church are meant to set a tone. The white and gold of Easter signify celebration and joy; the fire red of a martyr's feast stands for passion, blood, and fervor. Like ashes, Lenten purple is a sign of reflection and conversion. The purple of Lent is not the noble violet of royalty but rather the blue-purple of sober commitment.

Colors have cultural significance, yet cultures change as do technologies that control the ability to dye cloth. In the same way, the use of color has changed in the history of the Church. The practice familiar to present-day Roman Catholics began in twelfth-century

Rome and became the norm in the sixteenth-century reformed missal of Pope Saint Pius V.

Ashes: Sackcloth and ashes are ancient forms of repentance. Sackcloth, a coarse, uncomfortable cloth, is a sign of mourning. Jonah the prophet preached repentance to Nineveh, a pagan city. "When the news reached the king of Nineveh, he rose from his throne, laid aside his robe, covered himself with sackcloth, and sat in the ashes" (Jonah 3:6). He proclaimed a fast for all the people, directed that all the people and animals should be clothed in sackcloth and that everyone should turn from their evil ways.

Palms: On the Sunday before Easter, the beginning of Holy Week, we hold palms in our hands in imitation of the people of Jerusalem who welcomed Jesus and tore palm branches off the trees to throw in the path of the donkey he was riding. Like the strewing of flower petals in a dignitary's path, this was a sign of honor. Holding our palm branches gets us more involved in this week filled with powerful memories of Jesus' passion and death.

Yet, like fasting, these physical symbols of Lent can be abused. Jesus warned against external signs of religious practice that have no real connection to internal attitudes. Signs can be empty or "just for show." At the beginning of our Lenten journey as ashes are put on our foreheads, we are reminded to "remember you are dust and to dust you will return" or "repent and believe the good news." The ceremony of receiving ashes reminds us of our mortality and human weakness. It recalls for us, on Ash Wednesday, the constant need we have for conversion and reconciliation.

Holy Oils: The anointing of kings and priests in the Old Testament was symbolic of their having been chosen by God. In the First Book of Samuel we read of David's anointing. "[David] was ruddy, a youth handsome to behold and making a splendid appearance. The LORD said, 'There — anoint him, for this is he!' Then Samuel, with the horn of oil in hand, anointed him in the midst of his brothers; and from that day on, the spirit of the LORD rushed upon David" (1 Samuel 16:12-13).

Jesus' title of *Messiah,* the Hebrew term for "anointed," was translated into Greek as *Christos,* the word for "anointed one." When we say "Jesus Christ," we are saying "Jesus the anointed." Oil is still regarded as an agent for softening the skin or easing aching muscles. Our sacramental use of oil combines the ancient practice of anointing as a sign of selection with the association of oil with healing and strength.

The Mass of Chrism is generally celebrated on Holy Thursday morning by the bishop together with the priests and deacons of his diocese or archdiocese. During this liturgy, three types of oil are prepared for use in the sacraments of baptism, confirmation, holy orders, and the anointing of the sick during the coming year.

Chrism is the first oil prepared. Chrism contains olive oil and perfume taken from the balsam tree. This is the oil that clergy use for the anointings in baptism, confirmation, and the ordination of priests and bishops. In the consecratory prayer, the bishop asks that the gifts of the Holy Spirit be poured out on the brothers and sisters who will be anointed with this oil so their holiness will shine for all to see.

The Oil of Catechumens is blessed olive oil. The bishop prays that those anointed with it will have the wisdom and strength to continue their preparation for baptism. Adults preparing for baptism during the Easter Vigil are anointed to encourage and strengthen them in their decision. Infants are anointed just before they are baptized.

The Oil of the Sick is used in the sacrament of anointing of the sick. It is olive oil or other plant oil. Although there are circumstances in which the priest administering the sacrament may bless the oil himself, the bishop blesses a large quantity on Holy Thursday. He prays that the persons anointed with the oil will be "freed from pain and illness and be made well again in body, mind, and soul."

The Stations of the Cross and the Rosary

A friend who is not Catholic stopped for a visit at St. Patrick's Cathedral in New York City. Once inside, he observed two people walking around the church, with regular stops in front of pictures. Above each picture was a wooden cross. His curiosity led to an examination of the pictures and the discovery that they depicted Jesus' suffering and death.

As mysterious as all of this might have been for my friend, most Catholics readily associate the Stations of the Cross, or Way of the Cross, with Lent and Holy Week. Who doesn't remember the standing, genuflecting, and kneeling that accompany the pilgrimage from one station to the next?

This devotion was originally brought back

from the Holy Land by pilgrims who had meditated on Jesus' suffering as they walked from the Garden of Gethsemane to Calvary. After returning to their homes in Europe, some put up crosses or pictures or statues to remind them of Holy Land shrines. For those faithful who could not afford or endure travel to the Holy Land, these local symbols became their shrines for meditation.

In the sixteenth and seventeenth centuries, the Stations of the Cross as we know them today took form. The number of stations had varied, but eventually the present fourteen were accepted. The devotion spread through Germany, the Netherlands, Italy, France, and Spain. The Franciscans worked to establish the devotion and succeeded to the point where nearly every church and chapel had its set of fourteen crosses, with or without scenes from the passion.

Praying the stations requires only the meditative walk from one station to the next. No specific prayer format is required, though many have been written, perhaps the most familiar of which is the *Way of the Cross* by Saint Alphonsus Liguori. The gospel accounts of Christ's passion and death are also excellent guides to praying the stations.

The Stations of the Cross enable us to experience sorrow for sin and gratitude for forgiveness as we walk with Jesus from his trial before Pilate to his collapse under the weight of the cross, his meeting with Mary, his crucifixion, death, and burial.

A meditation on the sufferings of Jesus is also available in the Sorrowful Mysteries of the rosary: the Agony in the Garden, the Scourging at the Pillar, the Crowning With Thorns, the Carrying of the Cross, and the Crucifixion. Less well known is the Seven Dolor rosary with meditations on the sufferings Mary experienced during her life, most of which are during Jesus' passion. The Servite Fathers foster this devotion.

"Forgive Us Our Trespasses"

The Lord's Prayer is a constant reminder of our need for God's forgiveness and our obligation to extend that same forgiveness to those who offend us.

More than any other season, Lent focuses our attention on the reality of our human condition with all its failings, but also with all its potential. Lent has a way of reinforcing those refrains we so easily take for granted: "Lord have mercy," "I confess," "Let us call to mind our sins," and "Lamb of God...have mercy on us."

Reflection on these refrains is especially appropriate because Lent, besides being the time of final preparation for those who would be baptized at Easter, was once a time when sinners did public penance in view of being reconciled at the end of Lent. They would approach the bishop privately to confess their sins, which in the small, close communities of early Christianity were probably known to everyone anyway. At the beginning of Lent, the bishop would impose ashes on the penitents and give them a public penance to perform. Then at Easter they could receive the Eucharist as fully reconciled members of the Church. Lent has thus traditionally been connected with the sacrament of penance, or reconciliation.

Our frequent minor infractions, traditionally called "venial," are forgiven in many ways. There are prayer and meditation, the Act of Contrition, apologies to those we've hurt, making amends, acts of charity, the Eucharist, and the sacrament of penance. Regular confession is a devotional practice the Church recommends as a protection against serious sin. The grace of this sacrament, the examination of conscience and preparation to confess our sins, the reading of Scripture, and the advice of the confessor are all helps to spiritual growth.

The Church has always been concerned about those in serious sin. The Gospel of Matthew (see 18:15-17) and Paul's Second Letter to the Corinthians (see 2:5-11) show that concern in the way they deal with serious transgressions. In John 20:22-23, Jesus gives the Church its mandate to forgive sins.

The sacrament of penance is the Church's way of bestowing God's mercy on those who have sinned seriously after baptism or since their last confession. The priest or bishop, as the representative of Jesus and his people, gives an effective sign of forgiveness to those who repent.

We know that God forgives the person who sincerely repents. But we also know there is a human need for an external sign of that forgiveness. During Lent, most parishes provide a communal penance service, inviting all to individual confession and absolution of sins. Lent is a call to conversion, as we hear in the readings at Mass on Ash Wednesday. One way of deepening that conversion is through the sacrament of penance.

Daily Mass

A Lenten practice many people adopt is attendance at Mass every day or at least several days a week. Parishes usually add one or more daily Masses during Lent, usually at times that enable more people to attend. Early morning, noon, or evening are popular times for these extra Masses.

The passages selected for Lenten liturgies are chosen to deepen the various themes of Lent. Of course, being able to participate in the Eucharist daily is a great source of spiritual nourishment as well. Some people continue this practice after Lent is over, if they are able. If you cannot attend daily Mass, it is worthwhile to take fifteen to twenty minutes to reflect on the daily readings.

The Sacred Triduum

The entire period up to Easter Sunday was once popularly, but inaccurately, referred to as Lent. Liturgically, Lent ends before the eucharistic liturgy on Holy Thursday. Holy Thursday evening, Good Friday, and Holy Saturday are called the sacred triduum. The liturgical renewal that prepared for the Second Vatican Council and has been carried out since the Council has clarified the relationship between Lent and the sacred triduum.

The three days from Thursday through Holy Saturday — the sacred triduum — are the high point of the Church's liturgical year celebration. They form the solemn period for which Lent has been preparing us. It is unfortunate that many Catholics are uninformed about this brief, but important, liturgical season. Christmas, with its appealing story of a newborn baby, adoring shepherds, singing angels, and searching wise men, captures our imagination more than Easter does. Even Lent, with its forty days and emphasis on conversion and Jesus' suffering and death, is easier to grasp than the glory of the Resurrection and Easter.

At one time there was only the celebration of Holy Thursday, Good Friday, and the Easter Vigil, with a Mass during the day on Easter for those who wanted to attend again. In those early small communities, everyone gathered on Thursday, Friday, and Saturday from evening through to dawn. It was an experience of listening to Scripture, singing, baptizing new members, and glorying in the hope that enabled people in the catacombs to risk their careers, their fortunes, and their lives because of the hope they found in the death and resurrection of Jesus. Would that Lent could prepare us in such a way that we would have some of the same commitment those early Christians had!

The three days of the sacred triduum have their own special symbols. On Holy Thursday, we have the washing of the feet, a sign taken from Jesus' own action at the Last Supper in which he gave his disciples an example of service. At one time in the Church, this was considered a minor sacrament of the charity we should have for one another. On Good Friday, the Passion from the Gospel of John is read. In the exaltation of the cross on Good Friday, the cross is carried in procession while the priest gradually uncovers it, stopping three times. At each stop he sings, "This is the wood of the cross, on which hung the Savior of the world." After that, the cross is presented for individuals in the congregation to approach and venerate.

The Easter Vigil is filled with symbols. It begins in the evening with a dark church. All the old lights have been put out, and then a new light is kindled from flints. This fire, which is usually lit outside the church, signifies a new beginning. A beautiful song of praise is sung to God the creator and God the savior. Readings from the Scriptures follow, telling the story of salvation all the way to the Resurrection. A candle, the symbol of Christ, is decorated and plunged into the water that will be used for baptismal water. Oil and salt are poured into the water. Finally, that outstanding symbol of the Resurrection, the Alleluia, which was not heard all during Lent, is sung over and over. "The Mass is ended, go in peace, alleluia, alleluia." "Thanks be to God, alleluia, alleluia."

Our experience of Lent begins with ashes and words that call us sinners to repentance. Through the interior conversion to which it calls us, aided by the rich and varied symbols of the season, Lent prepares us to sing Alleluia wholeheartedly to our risen Lord at Easter.

More Lenten Resources From Liguori...

Day by Day Through Lent
Daniel L. Lowery, C.SS.R.

Reflections on the Scripture passages of the day, prayers, and suggestions for applying God's Word in daily life. **$4.95**

Living in the Light
Daily Reflections, Prayers, and Practices for Lent Cycles A, B, and C
Rev. Warren J. Savage and Mary Ann McSweeny

Based on the daily Scripture readings for Lent. Each day you focus on one scriptural theme through breaking open the Word, reflecting upon it, praying, and practicing what you learn. **$3.95**

The Stations of the Cross with Pope John Paul II
Rev. Joseph M. Champlin, illustrated by Grady Gunter

Adapts the Stations of the Cross from the ones used by Pope John Paul II at the Roman Colosseum on Good Friday, 1991. Based on the events in the Gospels, each station is accompanied by specific Gospel readings and each of the prayer responses is taken from a portion of the Psalms. **$2.95**

Building Family Faith Through Lent
Lectionary-Based Activities
by Lisa Bellecci-st.romain

Weekly sharing sessions, readings from each Sunday of Lent, prayers, and craft sessions provide the starting point for families to have fun during Lent while sharing spiritual values. Available for all 3 cycles. **$3.95**

Order from your local bookstore or write to
Liguori Publications
Box 060, Liguori, MO 63057-9999
*Please add 15% to your total for shipping and handling
($3.50 minimum, $15 maximum).*